Freemotion Quilting

Judy Woodworth

Located in Paducah, Kentucky, the American Quilter's Society (AQS) is dedicated to promoting the accomplishments of today's quilters. Through its publications and events, AQS strives to honor today's quiltmakers and their work and to inspire future creativity and innovation in quiltmaking.

Executive Editor: Andi Milam Reynolds
Senior Editor: Linda Baxter Lasco
Technical Editor: Marge Boyle
Graphic Design: Lynda Smith
Cover Design: Michael Buckingham
Studio Photography: Charles R. Lynch
How-To Photography: Judy Woodworth

Additional copies of this book may be ordered from the American Quilter's Society, PO Box 3290, Paducah, KY 42002-3290, or online at www. AmericanQuilter.com.

Text © 2010, Author, Judy Woodworth
Artwork © 2010, American Quilter's Society

Library of Congress Cataloging-in-Publication Data

Woodworth, Judy.
  Freemotion quilting / by Judy Woodworth.
    p. cm.
  ISBN 978-1-57432-671-0
  1. Crazy quilts--Design. 2. Patchwork quilts--Design.
3. Quilting. I.
Title.
  TT835.W6595 2010
  746.46--dc22

                              2010035271

American Quilter's Society
P. O. Box 3290 • Paducah, KY 42002-3290
www.AmericanQuilter.com

Proudly printed and bound in the United States of America

Right: BUTTERFLY MIGRATION, detail. Full quilt on page 52. Cover and title page: THREE GIRAFFES, details. Full quilt on page 67.

Dedication

This book is lovingly dedicated to my husband, Woody, my high-school sweetheart. He has encouraged me and been with me every step of the way—from hauling suitcases full of quilts, to helping me dye my fabric, and going with me to every quilt show. He completes me.

To my teachers— Judy Allen, Pam Clarke, Janet Fogg, Cathy Franks, Renae Haddadin, Karen McTavish, Sharon Schamber, and Linda Taylor—for all their encouragement and inspiration.

To my students. Their excitement is contagious.

Contents

$\mathcal{A}$ppreciation

ARABESQUE, details, pages 4–5. Designed and pieced by Mary Sue Suit and quilted by the author. Quilt photo on page 63.

I need to thank my best friends for sharing their quilts and for being such an important part of my life.

I met Mary Sue Suit about ten years ago and we found out that we lived a few blocks away from each other. She told me to call and she stormed into my life with kindness, inspiration, and motivation. We have been there for each other through trials and tribulations and our friendship just gets stronger and stronger. It's always fun to quilt with her. We have learned many things about doing show quilts including that sometimes our favorite quilts don't win anything. And that is a lesson of its own—just loving the process of doing the quilts together.

Mary Sue Suit

Photo by Consumer Programs Incororated d/b/a Picture Me! Portrait Studios

Thanks to Steve Anderson, Ron Parker, and all the people at Gammill® Quilting Systems who have supported me and been there for me in my quilting journey.

Joan Davis is the hardest-working woman I have ever known. Our friendship began when I taught for her at her first quilt shop. At the time I met her she had just gone through some health problems including

Joan Davis

Photo by Johnny Sundry

breast cancer. It would have sent most of us running into retirement. I was so impressed with her and her zest for life that it wasn't long before we became good friends and quilting partners.

My husband, Woody, has dyed and painted several of the quilts in this book. It has been fun working with him on this crazy quilting thing that I do. He is my best friend and lifelong partner. We made five beautiful babies together; Angie, Kim, Becky, Bill, and Melissa. They have married wonderful people and my grandchildren are precious. I appreciate their encouragement and participation in my quilting from modeling my wearable art to driving me to Denver with my quilting machine, doing my homepage, helping square up quilts, and designing quilts with me. They are my biggest cheerleaders. I love them all.

To Andi Reynolds, AQS executive book editor; Linda Baxter Lasco, senior editor; and Lynda Smith, graphic designer, for their help and belief in me.

$\mathscr{I}$ntroduction

From my early beginnings, I was a quilter with no confidence. I've come a long way to the bring-it-on attitude I have now. I hope to bring you along, help you to learn how to feel the joy, and to learn the skills so you can become the quilter you dream you can be.

I remember the first time that I quilted a free-motion feather with a double stem in a customer's solid-colored border. My heart raced; I took a couple of deep breaths. I hesitated ever so slightly before I started the gentle undulating stem. At the end of the stem I began to feather back to the beginning. Okay, not so bad. Now the double stem, with the goal to keep it a little less than ¼" from the first stem. I pushed the start button and quilted the second line. This time, not so good.

In fact my left brain, the analytical, think-everything-should-be-perfect side of my brain, started screaming, "Rip it out!" I decided to ignore the voice and turned up the music a little louder, hoping to coax the more creative, right side of my brain to engage and let me be more free-spirited. Relax. I quilted the feather back to the beginning. I took a step back and looked at the feathers from a distance. I'll never forget the joy I felt. It wasn't perfect but it was playful and fit the personality of the quilt.

The big test: my customer came to pick up the quilt. Her smile confirmed what I thought, and she even clapped her hands. I don't remember the actual quilt since I have quilted thousands since then, but I'll never forget the excitement I felt. It was as if a seed of creativity had been planted and I was truly "free at last."

My hope with this book is to make it as easy as possible for you to begin a journey of experimentation, whether you are a domestic, midarm, or longarm quilter. I will give you basic shapes and show you how to create many different designs. Your free-motion quilting will have its own unique personality. I have included many close-up photos of the actual quilting for inspiration.

Yes, inspiring you is my number one goal.

I didn't start quilting with confidence; in fact I almost quit right after I did my first quilt. But I found the courage to do free-motion quilting, enter shows, and even teach. Maybe you are sitting at your machine or standing at your longarm, and you are wondering if you could ever have the courage to quilt with total abandon, or if you could ever quilt anything good enough to put in a show. I say, "Yes, yes, yes! If I can do it, you can do it."

Free-motion quilting is about having the courage to quilt, with few or no markings, and letting the creative juices escape from deep inside you. You'll start with a few shapes that will explode and develop into original artwork completed on your quilt.

Good luck on your journey.

Chapter One:

*B*egin with Inspiration

One of the first things my students ask me is, "Are you an artist?" My initial response is to say no, I can't even draw stick people. But if I stop and think about the growth I have had in my quilting and drawing, I can say in a quiet little modest voice, "Yes, I am an artist." I will probably never be able to paint a portrait, but I can look at an inspiration, and draw the lines and shapes of a design. Not perfect, but good enough to help me capture ideas.

You can, too. You need to scribble, doodle, and draw, and draw, and draw until your brain can do it in your sleep. It's something to do when you are watching TV. Then when you get to the machine, you can draw with thread.

If you think you can never draw I highly recommend the book *Drawing on the Right Side of the Brain* by Betty Edwards. You can find it at the library. She explains that as children we learned to draw and enjoyed drawing until around age 9 or 10 when the critical, left side of the brain told us we didn't know how to draw. It's terrible. Many children just decide they weren't born with the ability to draw and quit drawing. Are you one of those?

I always thought that my husband and several of my five children were just gifted—that they were born with the ability to draw. But after talking with them, I discovered that they had been taught by good art teachers. They were shown how to draw the line, the

shade, and the curve of an object. In other words, with a little practice (or play), even an "I can't draw anything" adult could learn to draw.

If you break down a picture and only look at it in lines or shapes—such as a gentle curved line going up, or a straight line, or an oval shape with three little lines intersecting the oval on the top right side, or whatever you see—it will be easier for you to draw. For example, in the picture below, focus on the design that's at the top of this vase.

Inspired by the vase, I drew this quilting design.

Then I mixed it up and made it more free-motion friendly by repeating each arc with a space between. Echoing the arc eliminates any need to backtrack.

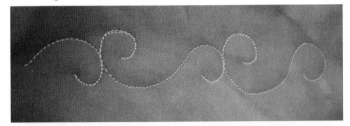

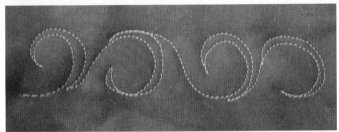

When you're drawing, turn on some music (or TV news) to keep the left/critical side of your brain busy (whichever works for you) and concentrate on the line. Think: "There is a gentle line that curves up, and at the top it starts to curl down and to the left in the shape of a backward c. The next line begins with a small c line and it gently curves down and gradually curves back up." Use a pencil to draw and bring your eraser. You can always fine-tune it. Some people find drawing with a Sharpie® marker easier to use as it glides smoothly.

You may never be a great artist (I know I am not) but you will be able to look at anything and draw lines that will get you started. Take your digital camera with you always, and some note cards in your purse, so while you are eating out, you can sketch designs you see on the ceiling or the carpet of the restaurant.

You are only going to be inspired by these items. You are not going to copy them exactly. In fact, because of copyright laws, you need to make them your own, as I have done in the drawings that follow. If the artwork is in the public domain because of its age or from a copyright-free book, you can copy it exactly. And, of course, pictures of nature taken in public spaces aren't copyrighted, so flash away. When you are walking by a stream, get an up-close picture of pebbles. It makes great backfill for your quilts. Keep your eyes open.

And for those students who ask, "How can I get inside your head?" look at the pictures and drawings and see how I am inspired. You and I are no different. Open up your eyes and see the possibilities. Surround yourself with inspiration. You can learn to draw and it will improve your quilting skills.

Gravesites are places to pay respect to those who have passed, and along the way be inspired by the beautiful carvings. Multiples of this design would make a great backfill—that is, a design to fill in the background areas of a quilt.

Inspiration is everywhere—even in an antique store where I found this leaf-shaped plate. I chose a different leaf shape but borrowed the vein lines from the plate.

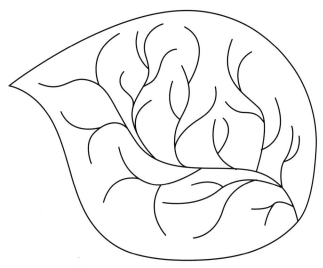

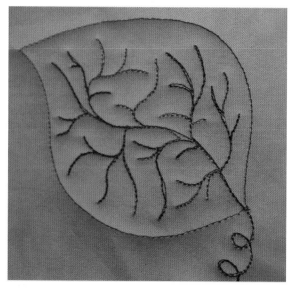

Draw your interpretation of a portion of the stonework. When you quilt it, feel free to change it as you go. Look back and forth from drawing to quilting and mix it up, add extra curls. This is free-motion quilting. No rules apply.

If you are nervous about free-motion quilting a design the first time, draw it onto the fabric with chalk or another marking device. Just be sure to test the marker on a scrap of the same fabric as is in the quilt to make sure that it shows enough to see, yet can easily be removed.

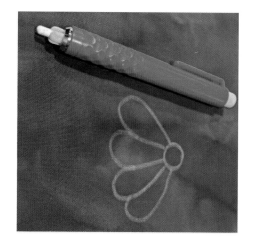

Try drawing a design inspired by a piece of wood filler.

The chalk drawing was done first, then the design was quilted.

This is an easier feather than the normal feather we quilt, and I'll show you how to do it in Chapter Four: Feathers, Please (page 29).

Keep a notebook for drawing ideas. This jar had a pickled leaf inside. I thought, "I'll put feathers inside of feathers."

From there I thought I would put the reversing curls inside of feathers. This idea was taken from the vase (page 6).

This design started with a photograph of a flower.

You can find backfill ideas everywhere, even on the bottom of shoes.

The above photo inspired this drawing.

$\int$tart Simple, Be Fearless

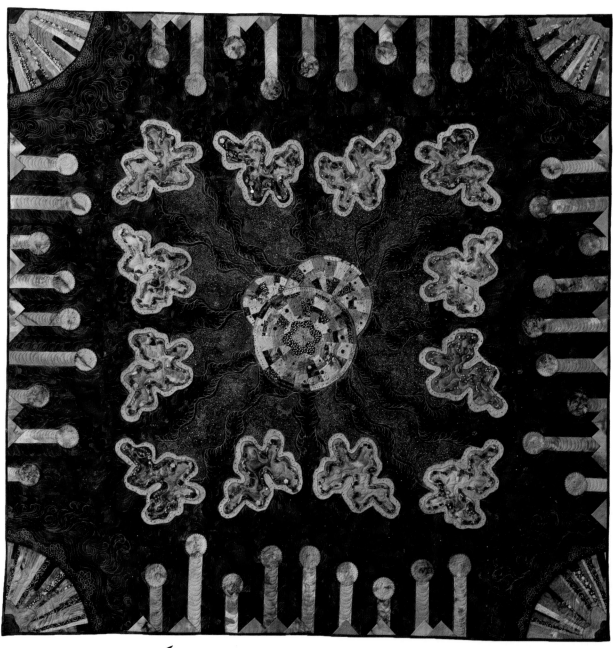

$\mathcal{A}$NNIVERSARY CELEBRATION
67" x 67". Original design by author, quilted by author.

If you are fairly new at quilting, or you are a more experienced quilter just warming up, you need some play time before you start your project. Pick some pretty solid colored fabric, cotton batting, and backing. Use a thin thread (such as Superior So Fine!™ thread) slightly darker than the fabric so you can see what you are doing, but not so heavy or dark that it shows up all your mistakes. Yes, everyone makes mistakes. Right now we are just learning to relax, have fun, and to quilt in rhythm.

If you have a quilt project you are about to start, make a sample sandwich out of the same fabric as the top and backing (sandwiched around a piece of the batting you intend to use) so you can experiment with different designs and colors of thread before you actually begin your quilting.

With my longarm machine, I will sometimes load my quilt slightly offset to the right, so that I have room to put in the practice fabric to the left of my quilt top. As I move the quilt down, I can stop and play with different ideas and threads and check my tension on the sample piece before I move over to the quilt top.

Making Quilting Decisions

Here are some things to consider as you plan the quilting for your quilt.

- What is the focal point?
- Is the design traditional or contemporary?
- Would an overall design or a variety of designs work better?
- What areas provide space for elaborate quilting?
- Where should the quilting be unobtrusive?
- What shapes in the quilt suggest backfill designs?
- What kind of batting is needed?
- Should threads match or contrast with the fabrics?

Different people have different ideas on what are the best choices. When I make these decisions, my number one goal is to enrich the quilt—to give it texture and interest. The quilting stitches will finally make it a quilt, make it come alive.

Many quilters have an identifiable style. For the most part, my quilting is subtle and in the background. There are only a few quilts where I want the quilting to take over. That is my style. What I hear and see when I quilt a top may be different from what you visualize.

There is no wrong or right way to quilt a top. It is whatever is pleasing to you. As in piecing, I believe repetition of elements is very important. Remember all the composition and design techniques that you used when making your quilt when you are making your quilting decisions.

Occasionally, the quilting is of primary importance in a quilt and the design of the piecing is deliberately made to show off the quilting. Think of all the simple Amish quilts with their lavish hand quilting. Think of those prizewinning quilts that cry out for wild threads and contemporary-style quilting designs.

When the piecing is traditional, complex, and detailed, the quilt needs lots of in-the-ditch stitching to showcase the intricate piecing and stabilize all three layers. The quilting is intense but is usually in the background, with matching thread (or a thread that blends). Again, this is your decision.

Basic Quilting Guidelines

• Ensure there are no thread nests on the back of the quilt by pulling the bobbin thread to the top and doing a series of tiny locking stitches as you start.

• The starts and stops should be nearly invisible with threads tied and buried or trimmed after the locking stitches are done.

• Balance the tension for good stitch formation. The threads should lock together in the batting. (See page 86.)

• The quilting should be in balance with a feeling of unity with good repetition.

• Make smooth quilting lines or sharp points when needed.

• Use stitch-in-the-ditch quilting to avoid distorting the straight lines of your border.

Remember to evenly distribute the quilting over the quilt. That doesn't mean you have to quilt an exact ½" apart over every inch of the quilt (although you could). It means that your areas of dense, medium, and light quilting should be spread evenly over the quilt. You are looking for balance and harmony.

Echo Meandering

To get my creative juices started, I always practice with echo meandering. I move gradually over the sample and then echo back to the beginning and take off to another area. Echoing the shape helps to fill the space and creates a lot of texture at the same time.

This type of large meandering can be used over a quick baby quilt using white thread. Most baby quilts are made with pastel colors, and since mixing color with white makes pastel, white thread blends beautifully.

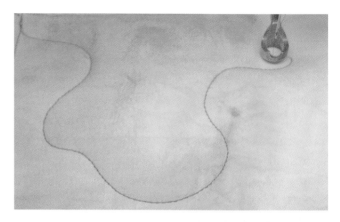

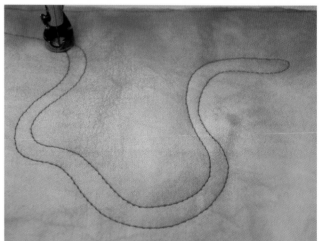

Ribbons

For practice I like doing ribbons with small circles, sometimes adding hearts. A feather is half of a heart, so it gets your mind thinking feathers before you ever get to them. At the end of the ribbon, reverse and quilt back staying about ¼" from the previous line (more or less is okay), or you can cross the line and make it look more three-dimensional. There is no right or wrong way, but try crossing the line after every convex bump.

Big e, Little e

Some people like doing "little e" and "big e" designs.

Waves

Some beginners find the wave pattern easy to execute. This is a small backwards "c." At the top, slide down (visualize a child's play slide) and start the next "c." It's great in skinny sashing or borders. Vary the pattern by changing the direction of every other wave, as shown here and on the next page.

To come up with different quilting ideas, sometimes I will take one simple shape and build on it. Here I have taken the traditional wave (the backwards "c") and tried to find as many ways as I can to quilt it. You can see how great these designs look when stitched.

MOUNTAIN, detail. Designed by Joan Davis, quilted by the author.

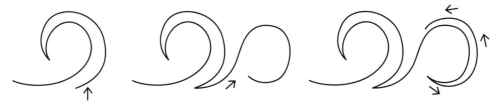

On this wave, come back to the base before forming the next one. Do not slide; instead, reverse direction.

Once you get the reverse action going you can add one or two tails.

Instead of a tail, form a circle at the end of a tail and quilt down the stem.

Now put a hat on it, rotating each "c" as before.

Once you get in a rhythm it's easy, but to get your brain and body to work with the reverse motion, it helps to say what you're doing out loud.

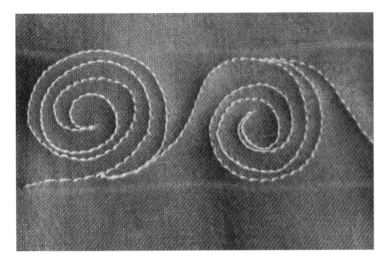

I encourage you to take any shape maybe a leaf, and see how many ways you can change its appearance.

KENDO, detail. Original design by Joan Davis, quilted by the author.

Teardrops

Then I like to practice teardrops, sometimes calling this my contemporary Baptist Fan. Teardrops can be echoed going outside or inside the first shape. I like to make a large teardrop on the edge of the border so that it fits exactly and then quilt the teardrops on the inside. When finished with the inside, I aim for the center at the bottom of the teardrop and begin my next teardrop, being sure to change the size of the teardrops from small to large for variety. To change directions, add a fourth teardrop.

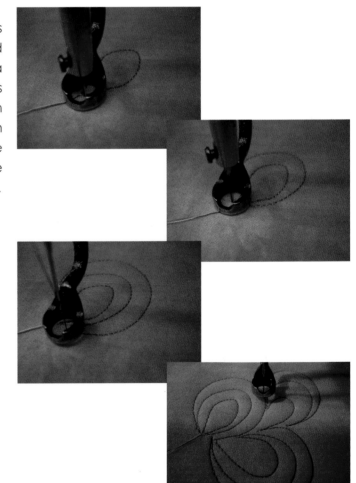

BUTTERFLY FANTASY, detail. Full quilt on page 95.

Half-Moons

Half-moons are my favorite backfill and are fun to practice. You can make them in a paisley shape with a more exaggerated curve on one side.

Whatever helps you remember in your brain so that it becomes easier to quilt is fine. This movement for most quilters is very relaxing, because you are rocking back and forth in half circles and you can make as many as you like. At the end of the row, change direction and go back the other way. It takes just a little practice and you can learn this quite easily.

When you quilt half-moons, practice stopping just short of the last quilted edge, trying not to cross through the previous quilting line. Focus your eyes exactly where you want to stop. This technique will also improve your feather-quilting skills. You can either purposely vary the space between each half-moon or try to make the spaces about the same. You can either start with a small teardrop and echo outward or start with a larger teardrop and echo smaller arcs inside the curve.

Half-moons

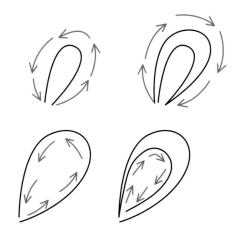

Igloo Echoing

Build on the half-moon shape by adding a short straight line before you make the next half circle.

Igloo echoing

Chapter Three:

Motion Explosion

The Color of Jazz
97" x 100". Machine pieced, appliquéd, and quilted by the author.

Motion, Pattern, and Movement

Let's talk about motion, rhythm, and balance. It's important to think about how your body and your mind need to work together as you're quilting. Yikes, that sounds scary! I'm not going to ask you to learn how to juggle, but in a way, quilting is like a balancing act.

You need to work on eye and hand coordination. If you are quilting on a domestic machine, gently glide and slightly grip the fabric with your fingertips, all the time trying not to tense up the muscles in your shoulders. You want to go at a consistent speed, yet sometimes speed up on curves or slow down so that your stitch remains even. You have to manage the bunched up fabric that you are not quilting, while a design or pattern materializes as you quilt.

On a longarm, you can't have a death grip on the handles. You have to learn to move on your feet as you are quilting across the quilt top without tripping. If you are sitting at or working on a domestic or longarm machine, you have to learn not to just move your hands and wrists. Sometimes when I am sitting I am wiggling in my seat to get just the right circle quilted. It's a complete body motion whether you stand or sit.

If you're standing at a longarm, it's like dancing. When I'm on my feet I will feel myself sometimes rotating on the balls of my feet, or moving my hips from side to side, while holding my elbows close to my body for more control. The longarm machine becomes your dancing partner, and you need a little rhythm to keep your quilting smooth and in control.

Both longarm and domestic machine quilting require that you learn to breathe and relax. You have to think about what you are quilting and where you are going next. And mostly you have to have fun. Otherwise, you might as well just hire someone to quilt for you and do what you like to do best instead. But I'm assuming, if you are reading this book, you really want to improve your quilting. I know you are probably tired of hearing people tell you it just takes a little practice. I say it takes a lot of playing time.

When I wanted to learn how to do little circles, one of my customer's Log Cabin quilts that was kind of falling apart at the seams was the perfect piece to try them on. I turned up the music to get in a rhythm and quilted circles over every seam until I was blue in the face. "No more circles," I shouted, but you can see that I've put all that practice to good use in a number of different settings.

ANNIVERSARY CELEBRATION, back detail. Full quilt on page 12.

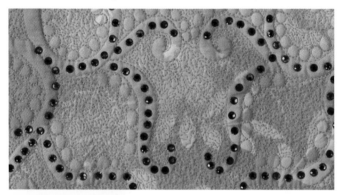

THE FRAGILE WORLD, detail. Full quilt on page 88.

SHIMMER, detail. Full quilt on page 47.

Rhythm

You may have noticed I have used the word "rhythm" several times. It must be important, huh? I am lucky, or old, I don't know which, but I learned to type in high school on one of those typewriters that when you got to the end of the carriage, you had to return it to the next line by pulling a lever across the top of the typewriter. My teacher believed that if we learned to type in time with music that it would help us to type faster.

The clicking of the typewriter keys, the music, and the swish of the lever created wonderful rhythm. While we were learning, the music was slower. Then the beat increased so that we were typing faster. This required typing words with our fingers while our eyes were already several words ahead down the line.

Quilting is a lot like typing. Most of the time, you will look where you want to go next and the quilting will follow the thought. That is the left brain and right brain working together.

The only exception to looking ahead is when you need to stop or hesitate so you don't cross through a line, such as when quilting feathers to a stem. Then glue your eyes to exactly where you want to stop. The eyes tell your hands, "Caution—you need to hit your mark."

When backtracking, focus right on the previously sewn line. But most of the time, when echoing or going to the top of a feather, look to where you want to go next and the quilting will follow the thought. Looking at the quilting foot and trying to space the quilting from the previous line just doesn't work.

If you have never tried quilting to music, it might help you to relax and enjoy quilting rather than dreading it. Depending on what I am doing, whether I am going slower or faster, I will play the music that works for the action. I know one quilter who quilts to hard rock. My guess is that she is giving her left brain something to listen to while she lets out the creative muse she definitely has inside of her.

When I quilted THE POWER OF A WAVE, I really wanted to create the feeling of power that water has, so I listened to the *Titanic* sound track over and over. I really think it helped me to conquer the passion of the wave.

The Best Part of Practice

As you play (or practice) you will find what motions, rhythm, and actions help you to quilt at your own special speed. You know what music you like to dance to with your machine, so listen to your inner beat.

This lily pad is full of motion and was free-motion quilted in water areas of THE FRAGILE WORLD (detail below). Try tracing this design with a pencil. Backtrack on the outside edge of the pad.

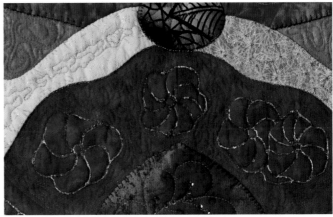

THE FRAGILE WORLD, detail. Full quilt on page 88.

THE POWER OF A WAVE
70½" x 74". Pieced, longarm quilted,
and embellished by the author.

Speed

If I move too slowly on a line, it starts wobbling all over the place. If I move at an even but faster speed I am able to echo my quilting, staying about the same distance away from the previous line of quilting.

Chapter Four:

Feathers, Please

Vespers

28" x 35". Original design by
Mary Sue Suit, quilted by the author.

I love feathers and will quilt free-motion feathers in just about every quilt I complete. There are many different types of feathers, all with different personalities.

I personally believe that you should learn every type of feather there is so that you have a bag full of feather tricks. Different quilts require different feathers. My husband used to coach soccer and basketball, and he always told the kids to learn to use both the left and right foot (or hand) equally well so they would be more complete athletes.

I think the same is true with feathers. Learn to quilt feathers forward and backwards, and learn to quilt feathers as backfill in every size and shape possible. It will make you a better quilter. Backtrack carefully and try not to cross through the stem line.

Longarm Feathers

A "longarm" feather is not exclusive to longarm quilters. It can be done on any kind of machine. It is more informal than a traditional feather. Each feather is either backtracked up the side or there is a slight gap between each feather.

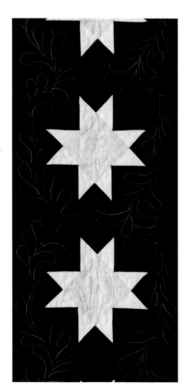

Playful longarm feathers quilted with variegated thread enhance the plain setting of the stars.

Cleveland, detail.
Pieced by Mary Sue Suit,
quilted by the author.

This longarm feather has been jived up with thread play.

Practicing the Longarm Feather

Practice drawing feathers before you try to quilt them. Get out some paper and a pencil and draw along with these instructions, remembering not to lift the pencil off the paper but draw continuously, just as you would quilt continuously. Then try quilting feathers on a sample sandwich on your machine—longarm, midarm, or domestic.

First, note that a feather is basically just a half-heart. Think "circle" at the top of the heart shape. Notice the slight curve near the point.

Start with the stem. Draw from top to bottom, then start your half-heart with a little inside curve.

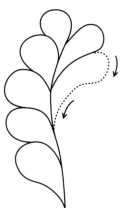

Continue making feathers up to the top of the stem. At the top of a longarm feather stem, switch sides and make feathers back down the stem.

Some people prefer starting both sides of their feather at the bottom of the stem. To get back to the bottom after completing the first side, double the stem going down and start the feathers going up again.

As you complete the last feather at the top of the stem, quilt tiny circles inside the double stem to get to the bottom.

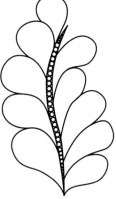

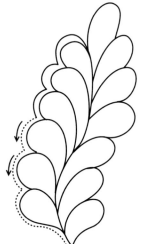

Try another feather. This time, instead of making a double stem, echo back down the first side of the feather, and then start your feathers going up the other side of the stem.

Bump Back Feathers

The more formal "bump back feather" (its invention is credited to Karen McTavish) mimics hand-quilted feathers. I especially love using these feathers when I need a long or more traditional-looking feather. These feathers backtrack along the tip of each feather, not along the sides.

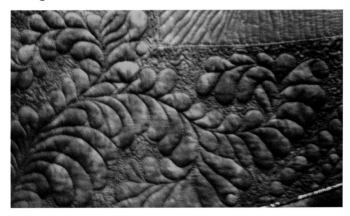

The Fragile World, detail, showing bump back feathers. Full quilt on page 88.

Feathers can be playful and filled with lots of threadwork, or you can put feathers inside of feathers as shown in Chapter One: Begin with Inspiration (page 10).

Practicing Bump Back Feathers

For a bump back feather, make your stem and first feather, then travel up the stem just a little and make a feather in reverse. Backtrack exactly along the top of the reverse feather. This is the bump back motion. Then make another feather in the same way

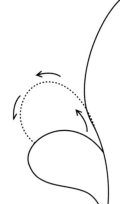

you made the first one. Every other feather is a reverse or bump back feather, backtracking over the tip to the next feather.

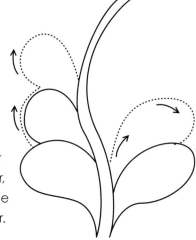

Practice drawing this feather with a pencil. Start at the top of the stem, draw down, and begin the feathers going up one side, backtracking along the edge of (between) each feather. At the top, draw the second stem line down and begin the feathers on the other side going up, or you can practice the bump back feather as explained on page 26.

Princess Feathers

These figures show how to quilt a Princess Feather, longarm style. But again, it can be done on any machine.

Start the stem at the bottom, ending at the top with the first feather.

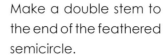

Start

Do feathers in reverse from top to bottom.

Make a double stem to the end of the feathered semicircle.

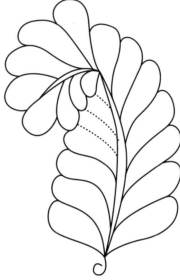

Feather back on the new stem and backtrack down the left side of the stem, creating the illusion of the feather going under the overhanging feathers.

Make a double stem back to the top, ending with a semi-circular curve.

End with leaves or swirls.

Make feathers back along the semicircle.

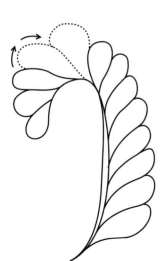

Contemporary Feathers

One of the most enjoyable things about quilting SAWDUST was doing the contemporary feather in the inner light-blue fabric. I chose not to do a traditional feather because Mary Sue had appliquéd feathers with bias strips, and I didn't want to do the same feather in blue because I wanted variety.

Start the slide back down, then bounce back up and kiss (barely touch) the top of the last line, then slide down the stem again.

For this variation, start at the bottom and quilt a stem with a curl at the top.

Bounce to the other side and slide down to the stem.

The real fun begins when you start mixing different feather motifs, adding extra flourishes as you go.

The completed feather

Slide down the stem and bounce up to the previous line. Kiss (barely touch) the line and bounce back down, remembering to slide down the stem each time.

At the bottom, add a few curls and then make a second stem. Tuck this stem under the upper curl.

SAWDUST, detail.

Advanced Feathers

This photo shows advanced feather quilting where one feather looks like it is tucked under another feather. Good backtracking skills are required but with practice and maybe the aid of a gadget ruler—if you are a longarmer, see Chapter 7: Structured Shapes with Gadgets (page 44)—you will be able to achieve this fun feather motif.

Practice this feather design with a pencil and paper after you see the process on the following pages. The feathers are done longarm-style, creating the stem going up and quilting the feathers by backtracking down the stem.

Now quilt feathers up the other side of the stem. At the top, backtrack down the single stem.

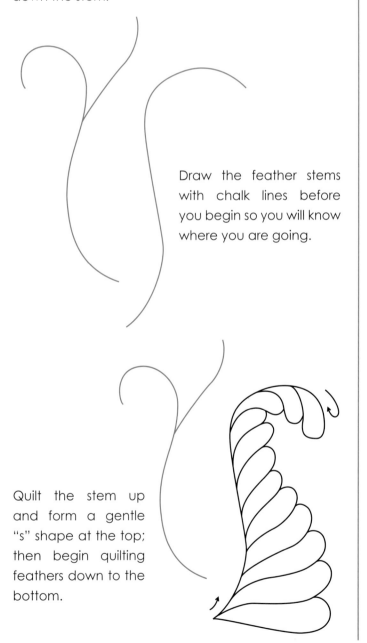

Draw the feather stems with chalk lines before you begin so you will know where you are going.

Quilt the stem up and form a gentle "s" shape at the top; then begin quilting feathers down to the bottom.

Backtrack through the bottom left feather and form a second stem that curves slightly out to the left, then gently back toward the first feather sewn. At the top, start the feathers going down the inside. The top feathers will look like they are tucked under the first feather plume. Either visualize that feather or use chalk or a purple disappearing pen to pre-draw the feathers as shown.

Only quilt the side of the feather, backtracking directly on top of the other feathers. This gives the illusion that one feather tucks under the other.

Backtrack up the second stem to the top and quilt feathers coming down. When you get to the other partial curly stem, quilt the stem and the top feathers until you meet the completed feathers. Then backtrack up the stem and complete the feathers down the main stem.

There are many different ways to quilt this advanced feather design. You could use double stems and do the bump back feather, which backtracks at the tip of every other feather as previously shown (page 26). You can quilt the standard longarm-style feather (pages 25–26); or if you like the longarm feather but only want to quilt your feathers going up the stem (instead of up on one side of the stem and down on the other), you can echo back outside the feather to get to the base.

Practice Motifs

Make copies of the motif below, and experiment with the different techniques described in this chapter to determine which you like best.

Chapter Five:

Spice It Up with Organic Shapes

Dog Days of Summer

29½" x 29½". Original design, pieced and quilted by the author.

Look to Nature

Nature is your best inspiration. This is the perfect time to look at all the photos you have taken of flowers, weeds, and other things of nature. Start designing organic shapes for your next contemporary quilt. Free-motion quilting is all about your creative visions.

Take any photo and simplify the image.

Your inspiration can take you to a new leaf. To create more interesting texture, leave every other space unquilted. This creates areas of negative and positive space.

I always have a sketchbook with me, and while I am watching TV I will draw designs I might use in a quilt. This snowflake was eventually quilted into BRILLIANT BLIZZARD.

BRILLIANT BLIZZARD, 68½" x 68½", and detail. Pieced and designed by Mary Sue Suit, quilted by the author.

Enhancing Organic Designs

When you do organic shapes, use contrasting thread that fits the personality of the quilt. ANNIVERSARY CELEBRATION is filled with free-motion organic shapes, done with over 20 different colors of thread. Notice how the light colors jump forward and the dark colors recede. You can control what shapes you feature through your thread color choices. Changing the scale of the quilting designs adds more texture to your quilt. I used three different colors of thread in one stipple cluster to create more interest,

ANNIVERSARY CELEBRATION, back. Quilt front on page 12.

Use bright thread on white or black fabric and tell yourself that it is just for fun. You don't even have to show it to anyone. When you give yourself permission to play, you will invent organic shapes that will excite you and you will use the shapes in a future quilt.

Each design you create can be taken to the next level with the addition of circles, curls, or swirls. Add extra flourishes at the tips of a fern-inspired design.

Dog Days of Summer, detail. Full quilt on page 32.

Outline a feather with circles. Here the design is enhanced with fabric paint, applied after the quilting was done.

Organic Wholecloth, 55" x 81", and detail. Free-motion quilted by the author, painted by Bill Woodworth.

Clowning Around, detail. Full quilt on page 54.

Auditioning Designs

Place a glass or specialty plastic sheet over your quilt and use a dry-erase marker to draw your organic shape before you quilt it so that you will see what it will look like on the actual quilt. Use batting at the edges to protect the quilt and be careful not to smear marker on the fabric.

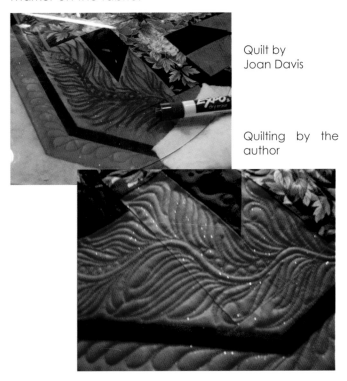

Quilt by Joan Davis

Quilting by the author

Joan Davis always gives me the green light to use organic shapes on her colorful art quilts.

RUNNING WILD AT SUNSET, 50" x 62". Pieced by Joan Davis, quilted by the author.

TWENTY THOUSAND LEAGUES, 49½" x 63". Pieced by Joan Davis, quilted by the author.

TWENTY THOUSAND LEAGUES, detail. Here circles are added around a floral design.

Because you can take pictures of nature almost everywhere, the organic quilting ideas will be plentiful. Remember to simplify your drawing. They don't even remotely have to look like the original picture. It is just your interpretation.

Start

Inspiration is everywhere. Even a simple sprout with leaves can lead to a design idea. Copy this page and trace over this plant stem design without lifting your pencil. Feel the freedom.

Chapter Six:

*C*enter Motifs

*R*OYAL PURPLE PASSION
Original wholecloth by the author, detail.

So many quilts have a perfect spot for a center motif. Feather motifs are my favorite, but I let the quilt tell me the best center design to use. The trick to quilting a design over any block, whether it is pieced or a blank canvas, is to get the right size motif for the space. The size depends on how heavily you are quilting the quilt.

If you are quilting lightly, then a well-centered motif with a little breathing room around it is just enough. If you are quilting heavily, you may wish to free-motion quilt the design and then put backfill around the motif. The fun of doing a free-motion design is that if the design looks too small for the space, you can just outline it several times until it is the perfect size. You don't have to resize a pattern.

I am sure you are thinking, "Oh yes, like I can just free-motion quilt a design and make it look like something without using a stencil!" That is just the left side of your brain interfering with our conversation. Remember, you have the freedom to improvise.

Draw a design several times on paper, then draw it using the auditioning, glass-over-the-quilt technique (page 36) to see how it looks. After you have drawn it that many times, you can easily do a quick quilting sample to see how it looks in thread. A domestic quilter can just move the quilt away from under the machine and put a 16" sample sandwich in. A midarm or longarm quilter can practice the design on a sample mounted beside the quilt, as explained in Chapter 2: Start Simple, Be Fearless (page 13).

Okay, you have drawn and sample quilted your design. Now take a big breath, relax, and quilt the motif on your quilt. If you decide to put a curl in as you go, or add a whoop-de-doo, it's okay. People enjoy the irregularity of an artist's design just as they appreciate handmade items. The individual uniqueness of your design is what gives it life and personality and sets it apart from those who are using computer-generated motifs.

Centering Your Design

Pam Clarke first taught me to use a chalk pad to pounce with a centering stencil. You can follow the chalk lines to help with the size and placement and stay somewhat consistent as you're quilting free-motion designs. "Somewhat" is the key word here; it won't be perfect but it will look great. The marks made by many of the chalk pads in use today are removable with steam, but be sure to test first and follow the manufacturer's instructions.

You don't need to mark the center lines in many pieced blocks because the divisions provided by the seam lines give you guidelines to "hit your marks." As you do more free-motion quilting, you will learn to estimate distances and sizes accurately.

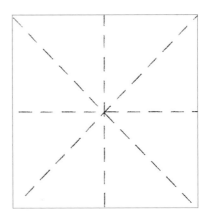

Easy Center Star

I like this star (or flower) design because only four lines of quilting cross in the center. Eight or more lines crossing in the center pile up too much thread in the middle of the design. To avoid that problem, the secondary star starts from the middle of the previously quilted star.

Center Motifs

This star may look hard, but it really isn't if you just take it a step at a time.

1. Mark the center and some guidelines to position the star. You can put a few chalk marks indicating where to stop at the tips.

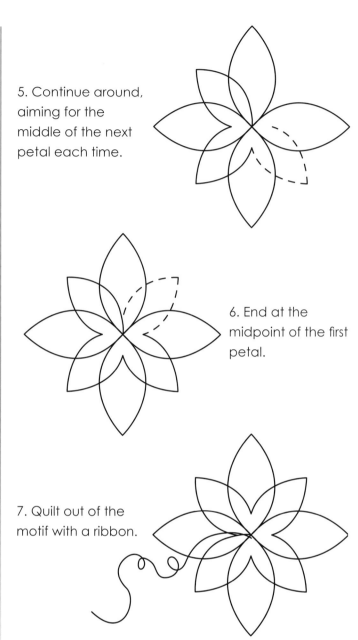

2. Make four star points (or leaf petals).

3. Go out from the center and quilt a second petal, starting in the center of one petal and ending in the center of the second petal.

4. Work to the next petal center.

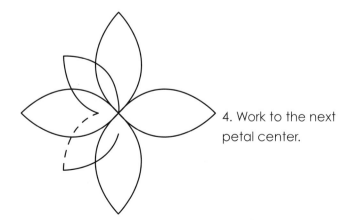

5. Continue around, aiming for the middle of the next petal each time.

6. End at the midpoint of the first petal.

7. Quilt out of the motif with a ribbon.

These flowers were quilted randomly with minimal crossing at the center eliminating extra thread bulk in the center.

BUTTERFLY FANTASY detail, 77½" x 77½". Made by the author. Full quilt on page 95.

Feathered Rose

I love Judy Allen's formal feathered rose stencils. I have used them many times but wanted to be able to do my own free-motion feathered rose. Inspired by Judy, I designed a simpler rose. I  decided the best way to exit the rose was to back out (or echo out) with an approximate ¼" echo outline.

Start echoing back out, putting a few leaves here or there.

Quilt semicircles around and around until you get to the center. Make a circle in the middle.

Echo around the outside edge, adding feathers and leaves as you fancy.

At different points along the way, a few leaves were added. Once you quilt to the outside of a motif, you can add leaves, feathers, or any fun thing that pops into your head.

Abstract Flowers

Janet Fogg first inspired me to quilt these abstract, one-of-a-kind flowers, and I thank her for encouraging my creativity.

Once you begin designing your own abstract flowers, you will never go back to stencils unless they're made from designs you drew yourself.

It is important as you quilt into the center and then exit to incorporate the entry quilting line into your motif. It will become almost invisible as you build your flower and finally exit.

Quilt into the center and form a circle; then in groups of two, form eight skinny leaves. The next layer is an indented petal with a soft inward curl in the middle. Continue around to the beginning entry quilting line.

Complete the four indented petals, then surround them with flame-looking leaves. This is where you can incorporate the quilted entry line into the design.

At the outside edge, stipple with a wavy single line, forming more impressions of petals. Giving a little breathing room around the flame leaves adds variety to the flower.

Creating different textures with soft and sharp points gives your free-motion quilting personality and interest.

The space between the wide echo is filled with circles.

Feather-like fronds center motif.

This center motif is surrounded by bump back feathers. You can see the backtracking along the top of every other feather.

Another center motif is surrounded by bump back feathers.

A wide stem area is filled with circles and curved crosshatching.

This is an advanced feather center motif and can be quilted as explained on page 31. Notice the feathers slipping under the other feathers.

Chapter Seven

Structured Shapes with Gadgets

Bouncing Bubbles
71½" X 87½". Pieced by Joan Davis, quilted by the author.

Gadgets are fiberglass shapes usually about ¼" in depth, held in place on the quilt so that the hopping foot on a longarm machine will not hop over the gadget as you quilt. There are hundreds of different shapes on the market.

By using gadgets, longarm quilters can have perfectly shaped skeletons for their creative designs. Domestic machine quilters can achieve the same result by using a water-soluble marker or a chalk pen and drawing around a gadget, round plate, or other round-shaped object. When you have the exact structure, for example a "perfect" circle, then you can be freer with your feathers or other shapes. Your eyes will register the "correctness" of the quilted circle even though your feathers are different sizes.

Gadgets sometimes move or slide as you quilt because they are smooth fiberglass. Apply small circles of sandpaper on the back or use rolled masking tape, sticky-side out. This keeps the circle or other gadget from moving.

Quilting a Circle

For longarm quilters, the trick to using a gadget is to move your fingers around it staying close to the edge. This keeps the gadget lying flat so that the machine's hopping foot will not jump up on it.

Domestic quilters may want to raise the feed dogs and quilt around a circle or shape before dropping the feed dogs and stitching their free-motion feathers. It will take some practice for any machine quilter to free-motion quilt circles.

When you quilt a circle, if you start at the bottom left side of the circle and move clockwise, you will be able to keep your fingers on the gadget at all times. You won't have to stop quilting, move your fingers, and start quilting again. Any time you stop and start quilting, you may have a change in your stitch length or a noticeable start and stop. So if you can quilt non-stop, you will have a better-quilted circle.

If you're quilting on a marked circle without a gadget, the direction you stitch doesn't matter. You can move clockwise or counterclockwise around the circle. The main thing is to try to quilt continuously as much as possible to eliminate stops and starts.

Bouncing Bubbles, detail. Full quilt on page 44.

Start stitching at "7 o'clock." Notice I am holding the thread tail with my little finger.

Spread your fingers and keep them close to the edge near the hopping foot.

Move around the circle. This is a small circle. On a larger circle you would need to move your fingers closer to the edge.

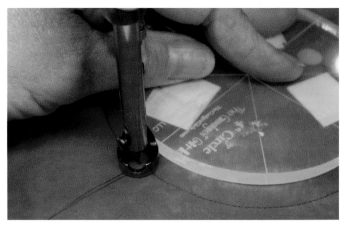

Finish the circle by moving your hand to the left and out of the way. Clip the thread and sew over a few of the beginning stitches. If it is a show quilt, tie off and bury the ends just as you would in hand quilting.

Doubling Up

Using two concentric circles of different sizes makes a positive space and brings the focus to the unquilted area of the two circles. The trick to using two circle gadgets is to line up the center points.

Use masking tape to stick the circle gadgets to the fabric; they must not move so that the circles are in exact alignment.

SHIMMER, detail. Full quilt on page 47.

BOUNCING BUBBLES, detail. Here two smaller circles were used within larger circles.

RADIANCE II, detail. Made by Joan Davis, quilted by the author.

SHIMMER, 25 ½" x 28 ½" and detail. Made by Mary Sue Suit, quilted by the author.

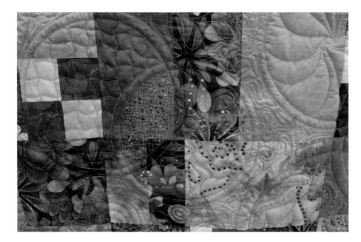

BOUNCING BUBBLES, detail. Full quilt on page 44. Here I used 5" and 6" circle gadgets. I like to create interesting freeform quilting inside the areas where the circles overlap.

SHIMMER, detail.

Adding Feathers to Circles

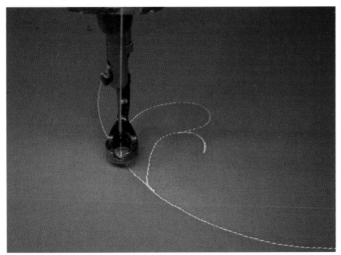

Start with a half-heart.

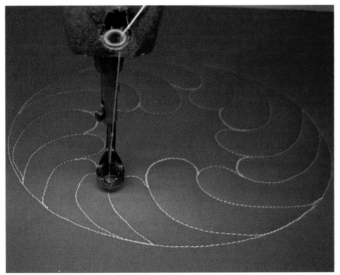

When you come back around, the head of the last feather can nestle into the first feather.

Visualize a circle in the indented area.

The completed feather has different sizes and shapes and is fun, but formal, because it is on a perfect circle.

Stitching a Heart

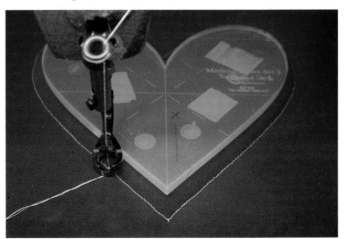

Start a heart in the same way you would a circle—at 7 o'clock. Put an extra stitch at the bottom point so that it is a point and not rounded off.

Try a heart-shaped wreath with feathers, surrounded by free-motion stippling. This quilted heart was completed using the bump back feather and the feather gadget.

Practicing the Heart Shape

If you are using a gadget, remember to start stitching the heart shape at 7 o'clock. On the heart line backtrack to the bottom and form the bottom teardrop. Make a feather in reverse using the bump back method. Then make a normal feather as shown, travel a little along the heart and form a feather in reverse. Connect to the previous feather and bump back, backtracking along the top edge of the feather. Form another feather. At the top of the heart, backtrack down the side of the heart and quilt the feathers on the right side. Try designing a new center.

Normal Feather

Bump Back

Bottom Teardrop

Bump Back

Other Shapes

On a long gadget you need to keep moving your fingers to keep the gadget stable.

The curve provides a sound structure, but then you can turn it into a funky, fun feather.

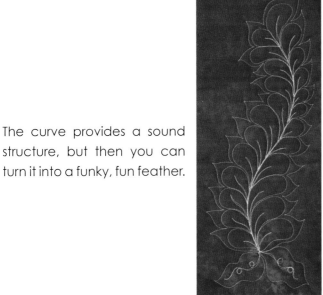

Use a swag gadget to establish the curve for a rose swag feather.

With some gadgets, you will need to keep moving your fingers around the gadget as you go because of an odd shape. You need to practice smooth starts and stops so that you don't quilt a jagged line. When you are new at using gadgets, it will only take one time for the foot to hop on the gadget for you to understand why you need to move your fingers. If it hops on your gadget, you might have to re-time your machine or at least change the needle.

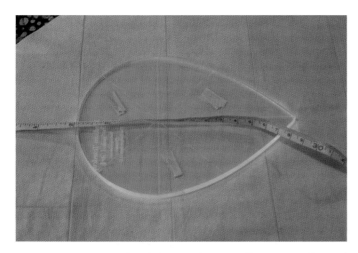

Measure your gadgets to make sure they are placed and centered the same way in every spot.

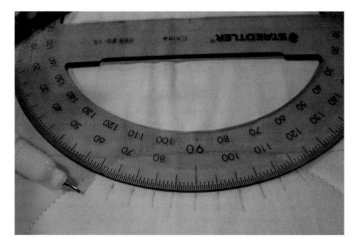

Quilt a teardrop shape. Use a protractor to mark equal divisions with a purple disappearing pen.

Use a ruler to quilt straight lines.

Now comes the fun part. Do a free-motion wavy line to create funky crosshatching.

Quilt feathers in a teardrop shape surrounding the first teardrop. On the inside feather wreath, use the little teardrop as a fence for perfect size feathers.

Chapter Eight

*B*ackfill That Makes the Quilt

*B*UTTERFLY MIGRATION
67" x 60". Designed and quilted by the author.

Some quilts do not have evenly spaced or sized blank areas. They are not symmetrical, but random in their design. These quilts lend themselves to free-motion backfill. When you do backfill, it's important to have evenly distributed areas of heavy, medium, and just a little lighter quilting over the quilt so that it will hang correctly.

Backfill Variety

Backfill can make or break a quilt. When you have a quilt that is fun and playful, select backfill that enriches the quilt and in some cases makes you laugh. The backfill in MR. PEACOCK reflects the natural effect of the feathers without actually being feathers. The green background has a hint of flowers and other natural shapes. Variety is the key to good backfill.

MR. PEACOCK, 84" x 99". Original design, appliquéd and quilted by the author.

MR. PEACOCK, detail

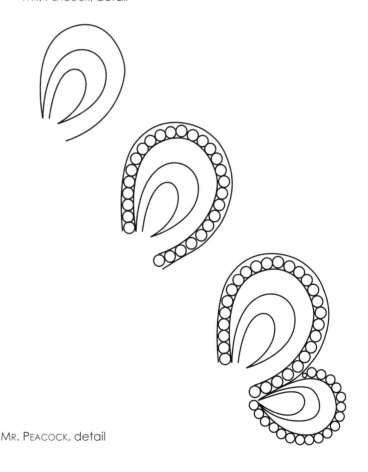

MR. PEACOCK, detail

CLOWNING AROUND, 62" x 50½". Painted by Bill Woodworth and quilted by the author.

CLOWNING AROUND was inspired by a photograph of our two daughters. When transferring the outlines of the clowns, I decided to improvise the backfill. The falling leaves are the ones shown in Chapter Four: Feathers, Please (page 29). The roses are similar to the roses in the rose swag feather (page 50).

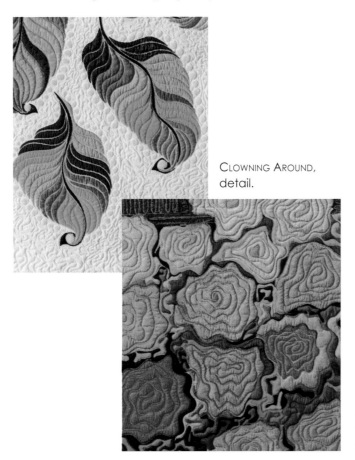

CLOWNING AROUND, detail.

Quilted wholecloth by the author, 20" x 18". Painted by Bill Woodworth. Sometimes stippling is perfect.

Stippled Backfill

Sometimes you can just do stippling to get the effect you want. To kick up the stippling in ANNIVERSARY CELEBRATION, I used three different colors of bright thread in each area. The different size and shape of the backfill gives interest to the quilt and draws in the viewer to study the quilt.

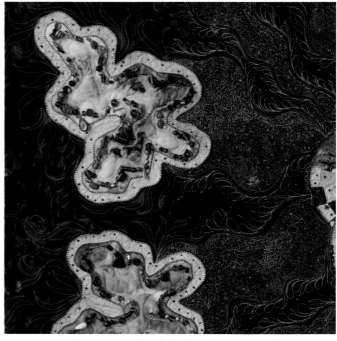

ANNIVERSARY CELEBRATION, detail. Full quilt on page 12.

Circles make backfill full of movement. On these leaves, I used six different colors of green to create depth.

BUTTERFLY MIGRATION, detail. Full quilt on page 52.

You can do some creative backfill on a quilt that is contemporary in design. Notice the curls that cross back over themselves. They are different sizes and curl in different directions. To separate an area, put four or five rows of echo quilting lines and even add in some circles.

ANNIVERSARY CELEBRATION, detail. Full quilt on page 12.

Adding circles, stippling, half moons, and sun rays gives a simple quilt interest, texture, and excitement. This small quilt was donated to the Nebraska State Guild auction to support the International Quilt Study program in Lincoln.

FEATHERS IN MY HEART, 20" x 20, detail. Quilted by the author. From the collection of Kellie Kachek of Ralston, Nebraska.

Some quilts require very little quilting. Echoing the ribbon (which in this case represents flight) and adding free-motion butterflies and dragonflies here and there was just enough for EAT YOUR FRUITS AND VEGGIES. The straight-line gadget was used to put the lines in the jar. I spaced them roughly ½" away from each other without measuring. With a little practice, you will learn to judge distance.

EAT YOUR FRUITS AND VEGGIES, 16" x 70", detail. Made by Gail Applegate, Sutherland, Nebraska; quilted by the author. Pattern from the Bottle Quilt Company Inc. See Resources.

GRAFFFITI, SUNFLOWERS & BRICKS

71" x 71". Painted by Bill Woodworth, designed and quilted by the author. The sharp, crisp lines of the overall design are softened by a mix of geometric and curved backfill designs.

Doodling contrasting shapes

GRAFFITI, SUNFLOWERS & BRICKS, detail.

Filling Negative Space

To create negative space on COLOR STAMPEDE (page 58), I sculptured around a whimsical design. Then I used different colors of thread to match each of the background fabrics so that the quilting wasn't distracting. Quilts need to include a place where the eye can rest.

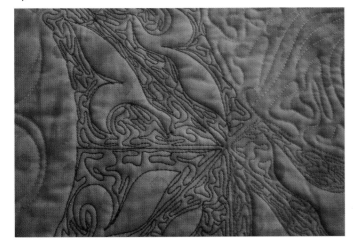

COLOR STAMPEDE, back detail. Full quilt on page 58.

In JUNGLE FEVER (page 68), an earthy free-motion design filled large open spaces. The same kind of backfill works well around feathers. I used Superior So Fine!™, Fil-Tec Glide™, and Aurifil® thread.

JUNGLE FEVER, detail. Pieced by Joan Davis, quilted by the author. Full quilt on page 68.

Thread Options

When I did the backfill on SWING ON A STAR (page 66), I couldn't get just the right color of thread, so I quilted it first in pink and then I went back and echoed the quilting in yellow thread. It was the perfect mixture of color. Instead of quilting two colors separately, some quilters will thread two different colors through one needle. To do that, use a larger needle than a single strand would require.

SWING ON A STAR, details. Full quilt on page 66.

These curly, swirly, winding leaves were done with a pale yellow matching thread. The design makes a great backfill or overall quilting choice.

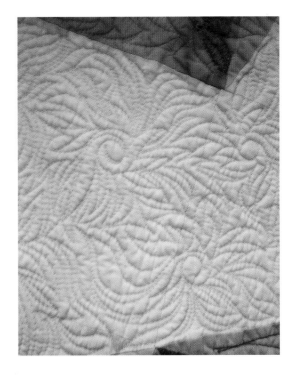

Joan Davis is standing in front of her original quilt COLOR STAMPEDE, quilted by the author. It was a finalist in the 2007 *$100,000 Quilting Challenge* magazine.

Because COLOR STAMPEDE is so busy, the kaleidoscope circles are quilted with a trilobal thread and the backgrounds are quilted in matching red, gold, and green thread to create only texture.

Developing Backfill Designs

There are countless options for backfill designs. Many of my designs begin as doodles. I'll often fill a page with one doodle after another, just to see what develops. Try your own doodles to develop new designs; then see how many of them you can work into your quilts. You may draw things you don't like but keep drawing. Fill up several pages. The more you put groupings of backfill together, the more you will find combinations that you like.

The following pages show a variety of backfills, from simple straight lines in a grid to more elaborate feathers. A variety of designs is more interesting than if you just quilt the same backfill design over and over again.

Even on a traditional quilt, there are many different ways to complete simple crosshatching. Have lines radiating out of the center, maybe add some curved crosshatching, or even a variety of stippling patterns to complement the straight lines.

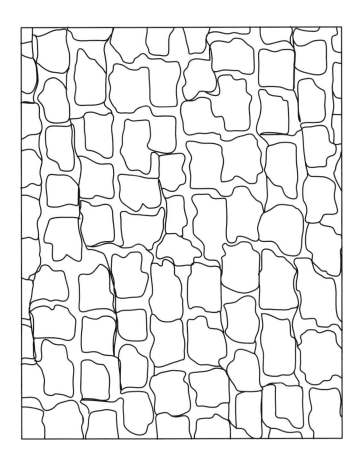

How Much Is Too Much?

How many different backfills can be put into one quilt? One very talented quilter did put in as many as 90! The average quilter would not do this. The trick is to maintain unity and balance, despite the variety of motifs and designs.

Let balance and repetition be your guide. The quilt will tell you how many different spaces can include fill, and that may limit the number of backfill designs you can use. Try to vary the size and scale of backfill, from micro (not a ton of it!) to small and medium-size, spread evenly over the quilt. If not spread evenly, the backfill will most likely cause distortion in some parts of the quilt.

You can partition off additional sections in a quilt to allow for different backfills by dividing areas with double straight (or wavy) lines.

A variety of teardrops, feathers, half-moons, and stippling backfill enhances the painted feathers.

Remember, backfill should enrich the quilt and give it texture and personality. But its most important job is to bring the viewer's eyes to the main features of the quilt, whether it is the quilted motifs, the appliqué, or the beautiful piecing.

A Gallery of Backfills

ARABESQUE, 90" x 90", Nebraska State Quilt Guild 2010 Raffle Quilt. Designed and made by Mary Sue Suit; quilted by the author.

ARABESQUE, detail. A mix of crosshatching and stippling creates a negative space design.

FEATHER DELIGHT, 20" x 30". Painted by Bill Woodworth, designed and quilted by the author. Notice the change in scale of the half moon design from the top to the bottom of the quilt, helping to anchor the overall design.

CARNIVAL, 69" x 70". Made by the author. Elaborate feathers surround the center while the ribbon candy design is repeated in the white rings.

CARNIVAL, detail. Straight line quilting sets off the center stippled petals.

SWING ON A STAR, above left, and detail. Pieced by Mary Sue Suit, appliquéd and quilted by the author.

THREE GIRAFFES, above right, and detail. Original design painted by Bill Woodworth and quilted by the author.

Chapter Nine:

ℬorders and Sashing with No Rules

𝒥ungle Fever

84" x 84". Traditional Lone Star with original design around star. Pieced by Joan Davis and quilted by the author.

Borders do not have to be boring or require that you measure everything out. Many times you can look at the blocks in the quilt and use that as a guide as to how many designs to put in each border section. And they are so much fun to do.

Border options are endless and just take a little imagination.

Simple Borders

To quilt railroad tracks, start with two lines in the center of the border. They don't have to be straight but can have a slight curve to them. When you get to the end of the first line, go down an inch or so and quilt backwards to the beginning. Then free-motion quilt the railroad ties.

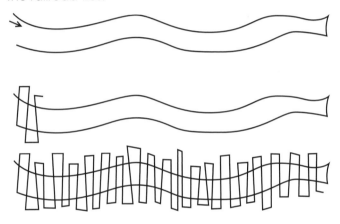

Use a ruler if you are uncomfortable free-motion quilting straight lines, but if you just hold your elbows close to your body and move your whole body up or down in a straight line, you will get a good line.

Another technique to use in borders or sashing is to simply quilt wavy, no-mark lines about $1/8"$–$1/4"$ apart with a short connector line at each end. They add wonderful texture and require no marking. Yay!

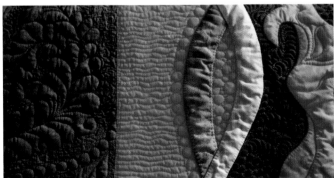

THE FRAGILE WORLD, detail. Full quilt on page 88.

In a set with blocks and sashing, do curly swirly designs in the sashing. Outline (or stitch in the ditch) around a block before you go into the block to do your design. As you finish quilting upward on a feather design, backtrack down the spine and create or echo down a curly swirly design at the base to get to the next block.

You could also use ribbons to go down skinny borders and sashing. To change direction, just echo back over the ribbon.

This curly swirly design is easier to complete quilting the design down on each side. The longarm machine setup rolls the quilt from the top down. Put a teardrop or corner design at the top corner, then begin quilting with the direction of the curls going in a downward motion. Normally you would "chase" a design in the same direction all around the quilt, but that doesn't work well because of the way this design is stitched.

I don't always use one color of thread and go non-stop echoing back to the beginning, but there are many quilts where a blendable thread can be quilted in both the sashing and the blocks. Sometimes you just have to change thread and do the block and sashing separately, because you can't find a thread that looks nice in both the border and in the block.

More Border Options

Quilt a line of leaves and curls across the border, then quilt the same leaves and curls backwards, leaving a small space between them to represent the stem.

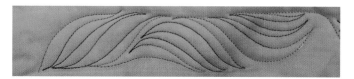

Quilt groups of three leaves, the first group from the top down, the second from the bottom up, and so on.

Curl into the center with swirling leaves in all directions, until you swirl to your next unit with a swirl to the middle. It looks hard, but it is very easy to do with a little practice.

This is similar to the first leaf border above, but instead of leaves, put in the half-closed circle, go back to the base, quilt to the opposite side, and repeat a half-closed circle. Notice the half-closed circles face each other.

Add fingers with a closed circle at the top. Change direction on the concave side.

Curved Designs

To mark guidelines for a curved design, use a flex-curve ruler, which you can purchase at sewing centers or office supply stores. Chalk some curvy lines in any direction. In the enclosed area, quilt some beautiful swirling feathers or other motifs.

If you are afraid to free-motion a feather grouping, draw it with a chalk pen until you get the confidence to quilt the feathers freehand.

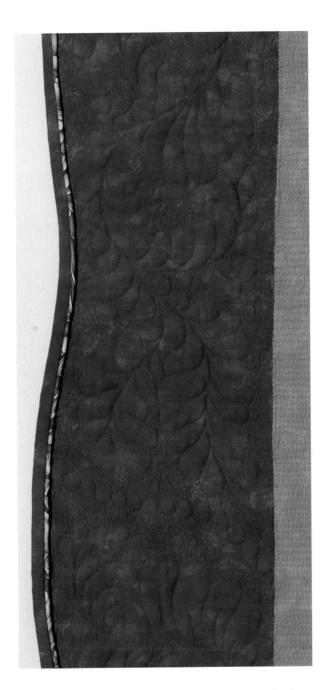

On THE FRAGILE WORLD (page 88), I tried my design out a few times before I quilted the rest of the feathers freehand.

Practice Designs

Copy and practice tracing over these designs with a pencil. Do not stop or lift the pencil. Try to develop a smooth rhythm from the beginning to the end of the designs. Then try quilting them on a practice sandwich. Mark off different width "borders" and try changing the scale of the designs.

Reverse back

Start

Start

Start

Start

Start

Start

Chapter Ten:

*W*hat and Where to Quilt

*P*ARROT'S *P*ARADISE
60" x 84". Hand appliquéd and quilted by the author.

When your quilt top is finished, the loose threads are trimmed, and the seams are checked and secure, it's time to quilt. Quilting is my favorite thing—creating "music" with the stitches.

Stitch-in-the-Ditch Quilting

Why do we use stitch-in-the-ditch in free-motion quilting? If you do the stitch in-the-ditch quilting first to outline blocks or shapes in your quilt, it provides good structure to the quilt. It prevents distortion from the free-motion quilting and allows the quilt to hang without pleats or puckers, even with medium-to-heavy quilting.

When I first told my customers that I was going to become an expert in stitch-in-the-ditch work, they all said they liked my curls and swirls. However, the ditch work complements the free-motion quilting. I could do wavy lines around the blocks (and might on a baby quilt), but it's just as easy now to use a ruler and quilt a straight line right in the ditch.

Subtle Quilting Stays in the Background

This is an example of using matching thread—in this case, beige thread on the beige background. The quilting still shows up but it doesn't take your eyes off the star.

Oregon Trail Raffle Quilt, 90" x 90", and detail. Pieced by Sharon Armstrong and the members of the Panhandle Quilt Guild of Nebraska, quilted by the author. From a Judy Niemeyer pattern, see Resources (page 93).

In PARROT'S PARADISE, the contours of the body are quilted with matching thread everywhere, as was the appliqué. This meant changing the thread several dozen times, but it ensured having just the right thread to blend and not show. The quilt is so busy, I didn't want the quilting to create more confusion.

PARROT'S PARADISE detail. Full quilt on page 74.

PARROT'S PARADISE was made in 2001. I tried to quilt around all of the apples in the border, but I don't believe I quilted it heavily enough compared to the rest of the quilt. This kind of thing you will learn as you are on your quilting journey.

During this time in my quilting, I was only using 100 percent cotton thread. Today I would probably use silk, Superior Threads So Fine!, Aurifil thread, or Fil-Tec Glide thread to match the fabric.

Auditioning Designs

I laid a clear, heavyweight vinyl over SOUTH OF MY BORDER to practice and decide what I was going to do on the diagonal border.

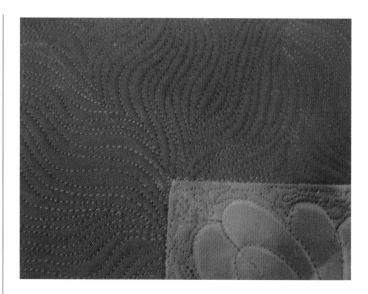

SOUTH OF MY BORDER, detail, showing wood bark backfill.

Positive and Negative Spaces Add Dimension

Quilting can add dimension to your quilt. Most times, anything you leave unquilted is a focus area. In SOUTH OF MY BORDER, this flower was too big to leave unquilted, so I stipple quilted the edges with a shiny thin variegated thread and left areas of unquilted space within the flower. The combination of negative and positive spaces gives the flower focus and dimension.

SOUTH OF MY BORDER, back.

SOUTH OF MY BORDER, detail, showing the partially quilted flower. Notice the variety of backfill designs surrounding it.

SOUTH OF MY BORDER, 60" x 71". Original design by Mary Sue Suit, quilted by the author.

What and Where to Quilt

The quilting is very much in the background on BRILLIANT BLIZZARD, designed and pieced by Mary Sue Suit for the Burgoyne Surrounded: New Quilts from an Old Favorite contest sponsored by The National Quilt Museum in 2009. There is so much color and activity in this quilt that the quilting needed to be dense, but still discreet. Some other quilters might have used more glitzy thread, but I loved the way this quilt looked and I did not want to change it with excess in-your-face quilting.

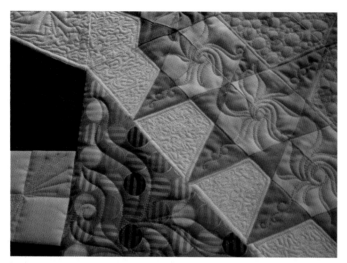

BRILLIANT BLIZZARD, detail.

I even ripped out a whole row of background fill in variegated thread, because it was taking over the quilt. I had tested the thread on a dark-blue fabric sample. It looked good in the sample, but on the actual quilt it was just too much.

Any area you compress with dense quilting becomes a negative space, which relegates it to an area of unimportance. In those areas I used Aurifil thread in matching colors with stippling, pebbles, and a medium curling star, all evenly distributed over the quilt.

In pictorial quilts, quilt to emulate the actual item, such as clouds and rippling water. However, when I did the flowers in SOUL MATES, there are pebbles for texture. These are make-believe flowers so I could do fantasy quilting in them. In-the-ditch quilting surrounds all the flowers and the bias strips.

SOUL MATES, 25" x 39". Pieced by Mary Sue Suit, quilted by the author.

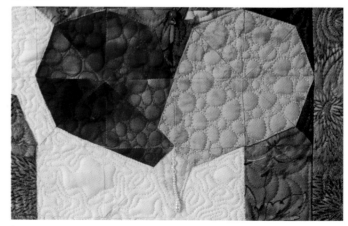

SOUL MATES, detail, showing fantasy flowers and pebbles for texture.

PEAR TREE SANCTUARY, 29" x 29", is an original design, appliquéd and quilted by the author.

I used YLI Fine Metallic Thread inside and around the leaves. This thread stays in the background but still adds a touch of warmth.

Background Fill

PAISLEY DAISLEY is a case of using formal feathers as a great background fill. Berries, half moons, and stippling give the quilt interest. In this case, I wanted the quilting to have a major effect on the quilt. It contained large areas to show off the quilting, which was done with fine Aurifil thread, and Sulky® variegated and rayon threads for the center flowers.

PAISLEY DAISLEY detail, 27" x 36". Made by Mary Sue Suit, quilted by the author.

PEAR TREE SANCTUARY, details, showing how the backfill mimics the leaves.

Matching the Quilting to the Quilt

My Self Portrait was designed for the theme category "But Is It Art?" at the Machine Quilter's Showcase in 2002. My interpretation of Picasso was fun and the beginning of quilting my crazy swirling stars in the background fabric. It was not clouds or sun rays—just a fun way to create movement, and it went with the personality of this quilt.

My Self Portrait, and detail, showing swirly stars.

(Trip Around the World) in 80 Days, detail. Full quilt on page 83.

In studying composition and design, I found that many artists believe you should never put anything of importance in the left-top quadrant of the art. This is something I pay attention to in quilting, but every once in a while I'll break the rule. I quilted a whimsical figure blowing hot air with metallic thread. At the quilt show I stood quietly to see if anyone would notice the wind. Very few people did.

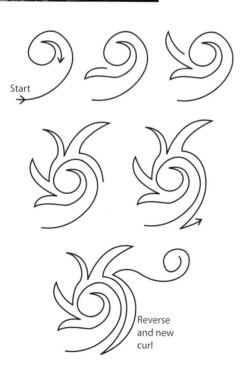

Start

Reverse and new curl

(Trip Around the World) in 80 Days, detail. Changing thread to match the colors of the quilt.

Interweaving Feathers

SOUTH OF MY BORDER, back detail, showing the interweaving feathers. Full quilt on page 77.

For the free-motion interweaving feathers, first chalk evenly spaced circles, then chalk in the stem line. You can cut adding machine tape the exact size of your border, then fold in half, again and again until you get the spacing you want.

First quilt the stem in the gentle curve. At the top, reverse the stem back to form a double stem. Begin doing feathers on the lower inside. When you have feathers to the top of the stem, do a wavy line or small circles down the double stem. At the bottom, start feathers up again and finish that side of feathers. Stipple back to the next stem close to the feathers and in the circle. Quilt the next stem and repeat.

Different quilts require unique quilting. I can't tell you what to quilt. It's something you have to decide for yourself. It is your personal style—your quilting voice. I encourage you to experiment and find that joy in each quilt.

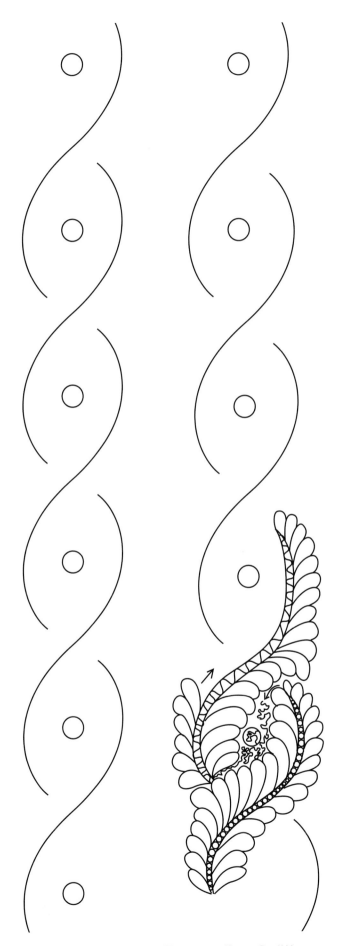

Chapter Eleven

Allover Quilting: Truly Free at Last

Judy's Bargello

41½" x 64". Designed and quilted by the author.

You don't have to quilt a pantograph pattern or a straight-line design to accomplish allover quilting. Bargello quilts are excellent candidates for curls and swirls in an allover design. Simply follow the path of the bargello with your quilting.

On (Trip Around the World) in 80 Days (above), I did an allover design in each colored area using matching thread for each section. If I had used just one color of thread, it would have competed with the colors of the many lights and darks. I was able to enrich the quilt without the quilting designs taking over the quilt.

If you get stuck trying to decide what thread colors to use in an allover design, look to nature for clues. For example, in this photo, the white of the lily looks beautiful surrounded by the greens of the leaves. Mimic that combination of colors in your quilting

Many times I have picked a white silk thread or white Superior So Fine! thread to use on true green, or blue, or even red fabric. Superior Threads Nature Colors™ gold, mustard, and wheat colors work well in allover quilting, even on a quilt that has a white background. Taupe blends beautifully in country-style quilts. Experiment on a practice piece to see what thread choices and colors enhance your quilt.

Chapter Twelve:

Thread, Thread Tension, and Batting

We are lucky to have so many choices of thread and batting. Everyone has their favorites but I encourage you to try everything at least a couple of times. Certain quilts will cry out for those glitzy threads while others may require cotton.

Threads

Some thread is thinner (lighter in weight), more delicate, and blends into the fabric. Others are heavy-weight cotton, maybe even neon in color. They shout, "Look at me!" I have more thread in my collection than I have fabric, and from just about every thread manufacturer, too.

I store large spools in pint-size plastic bags. It keeps the thread tails from tangling with other thread and keeps dust off the spools. I don't refrigerate them or store them with a wet sponge as some quilters do (the theory being that the moisture keeps the threads from becoming brittle). I just throw the bags in big plastic bins, roughly organized by manufacturer or type.

My workhorse thread for most quilts is Superior Threads So Fine! (50 wt.) on top, with Superior Threads Bottom Line™ (60 wt.) in my bobbin if I can find a good match with the top thread. The higher the weight number, the thinner the thread. Especially when you're quilting heavily, you don't want the thread to add extra bulk.

I use A&E® Signature® thread (various weights but usually 40 wt.) or Aurifil (50 wt.) thread for quilts that require the traditional cotton. I use YLI Silk Sparkle (#100 wt), and Fil-Tec Glide Trilobal 40 wt. thread for my show quilts. But these are not absolute rules. I will use whatever thread is perfect for the quilt. The only way you will know what thread to use is to experiment.

It's important to try the thread spool positioned both vertically and horizontally to see which way the thread feeds best on your machine. And yes, every machine is different. On my commercial longarm machine, I have the most trouble with rayon thread, but on my domestic machine, rayon works like a dream.

It's important to choose a needle with an eye that comfortably accommodates the weight of the thread.

Superior Threads provides loads of detailed information on their website including reference guides for both home and longarm machines that include needle size recommendations and a thread selection guide (see Resources, page 93).

Give yourself plenty of options when it comes to thread. Experiment on a sample sandwich before you begin.

Thread Color

The thread color is important. You can actually change the color of the fabric or change the personality of the fabric if you quilt with a contrasting thread. This may or may not be the look you're going for. On one of my earlier quilts, a Double Irish Chain with jewel-colored fabrics and white background, I used variegated thread on the whole quilt. That thread changed the color of the white and I didn't like it. Now, I rarely quilt on white or beige background fabric with anything other than white or beige thread.

In other instances, you may want to change the look of the fabric. Choose a thread that matches the surrounding fabrics when quilting a white area.

Choose gold rayon thread for tight, dense background quilting on dark or black backgrounds. It warms the quilt and shows off the quilting.

Trilobal thread, sometimes in a contrasting color, blends nicely and gives a warm glow without changing the color or value of the fabric. It does not take over the quilt.

Micro-stippling can completely change or block out the color of the fabric and affect the value.

Test the quilting on a sample made with the same fabrics as your quilt to see the effect of the thread and your chosen quilting pattern

My little Boston terrier, Lady, sleeps under my quilting machine and I ask her questions all the time. "What thread should I use? Do you think this batting is too heavy? What design should I use?" She just looks at me, as if she is telling me to trust my instincts. Maybe you should talk with your pet, and then trust your gut feelings and go for it.

Thread Tension

Learn to adjust the tension on both the top and bobbin thread if you want to play with the different weights and types of threads. If you are afraid of adjusting your bobbin tension too much, just buy an extra bobbin case. It will be a good investment.

The figures below will help you determine when and where to adjust your tension. Also use the Towa Bobbin Case Tension Gauge to get the perfect tension (see Resources, page 93).

Batting

Batting is another one of those things that can make or break a quilt. I'll give you some suggestions, but you should make up samples with the different battings. Almost all manufacturers have sample kits, so try them out. Quilt with them, wash one sample and don't wash the other—see what results you get.

Okay here we go...my personal preferences:

Antique-looking quilts or country-style quilts (reds, browns, and golds) look great with a good 80/20 cotton/polyester batting, natural or bleached. This is a workhorse batting. It washes up nicely, creating small puckers like on an antique quilt. It's fairly light in weight and perfect for bed quilts.

On my show quilts I like using two battings—the thinnest, most drapeable cotton in combination with a wool or silk batting. The cotton acts like stabilizer, enhancing the stitching. I usually like bleached cotton with a light scrim so it doesn't migrate out of the backing. If the backing is black or very dark I may even use black cotton batting. On a domestic quilting machine you probably only want to use one batt so you don't have to deal with the extra bulk. Try wool, silk, 80/20, 100 percent cotton, or a good poly.

If I have a quilt that is very light or it has white fabric, I will never, ever use natural cotton batting of any kind. The natural cottonseed oil can stain the light fabric. Some people don't like bleached cotton because of

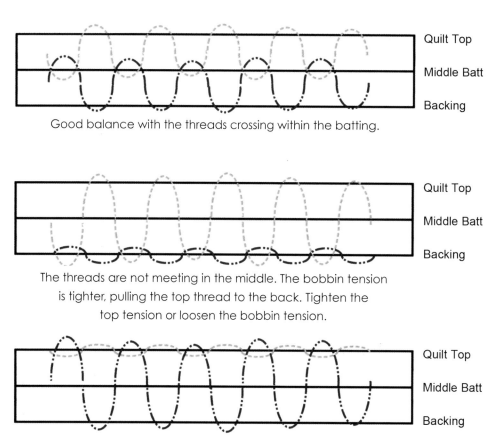

Good balance with the threads crossing within the batting.

The threads are not meeting in the middle. The bobbin tension is tighter, pulling the top thread to the back. Tighten the top tension or loosen the bobbin tension.

The top tension is tighter and is pulling the bobbin thread to the top. Loosen the top tension or tighten the bobbin tension.

the chemicals, but I use bleached batting in white quilts. Natural batting can be used where the quilt colors are darker and won't show stains. Remember, these are my preferences. Try different types to see how they work for you and the style of quilts you make.

When you use a wool batt (which is very light in weight) in combination with the cotton batting, the free-motion quilting creates a faux trapunto effect. The wool can quilt down to almost nothing if you heavily quilt next to a motif, but in the unquilted area it fills the space. When it gets wet, the wool puffs right back up. When you fold up a quilt to mail it, when it is opened and hung, within a few minutes all the creases will come out of the quilt. I sometimes use silk batting when I want a very flat quilt with no peaks and valleys.

Some quilters show their spotless, organized sewing room. Oops! I would rather spend time quilting or sewing than organizing. I sweep my floors and keep my sewing machines cleaned and oiled every day. Once a month I try to find the bottom of the table. I do know about where everything is located. If I can't find what I need, I stop and organize. Otherwise, it's quilting full speed ahead.

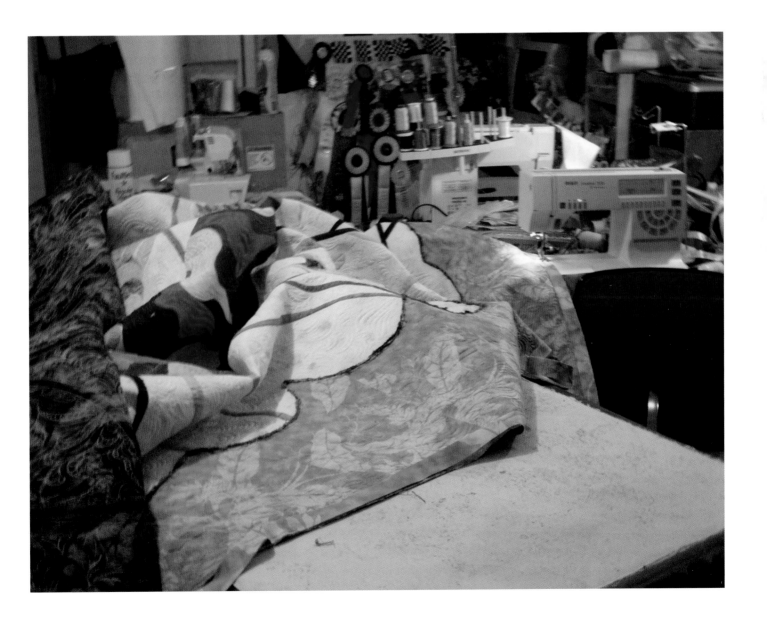

Chapter Thirteen:

Finishing the Quilt

THE FRAGILE WORLD

80" x 80". Original design by author.

After you complete the quilting on your beautiful free-motion quilted quilt, you need to finish it in the most professional manner you can (unless, of course, you're doing a funky art quilt with a fused binding). Just because you have not marked your quilt and it is full of curvy swirls and fantasy flowers doesn't mean you should take short cuts.

Blocking

Domestic and longarm quilted quilts should be blocked if there is any distortion and there usually is. Try blocking with one of these three methods before squaring up the top:

Use Method One if the fabrics have not been washed. Lay the quilt flat on two or three banquet tables (available from Sam's Club® and "big box" stores). Fill your iron with clean water and test it to make sure it is not dripping or dirty. Then steam every inch of the quilt holding the iron just inches above it. Let it dry an hour and steam it again, and then again, until it lies perfectly flat. Let it dry thoroughly.

Method Two uses a sprayed water technique and can be used when the fabrics have been prewashed. Lay the quilt flat on the banquet tables. Purchase a water spray dispenser like you use for plants. You can find it in the gardening section of any department store. Fill the plastic sprayer with cold water and use the pump to spray water over the entire quilt until it is saturated. Let it dry thoroughly.

Method Three is my preferred method for quilts with prewashed fabrics. I put the quilt in the washing machine on a gentle cycle with cold water. After the rinse cycle, let it go through a few minutes of spin. Carefully lift it out and lay it on the banquet tables. Smooth the quilt and almost lovingly caress it until it is perfectly flat. Let it dry completely. This will take 24 to 48 hours.

I'll put two fans on and if it's winter, I'll turn on a space heater (not too close to the quilt!), since my tables are set up in my garage.

A pieced quilt needs to be laid perfectly straight. Put insulation foam board on the tables and pin a new plastic paint drop cloth to the foam. Lay the quilt on top and have a partner help you to measure the quilt every few inches so that it lies perfectly straight. Pin the quilt to the foam board as you measure. Quilts with piecing all the way to the edge can't be trimmed, so you must pull and pin to the exact measurement you want. This can be done with a washed quilt or the water spraying method. If you are steaming the quilt, pin it first to the exact measurement and then do the steaming.

Squaring Up

By letting the top lie naturally flat and then cutting to square it, the quilt will really hang nicely.

I use every square tool I can find including my T-square, which is dedicated for my quilting only.

Four 8' x 2" x ½" boards that are perfectly straight can really help on large quilts. Use large square rulers in the corners.

Have someone help you measure every few inches up and down the quilt across the width and the length, from corner to corner. These must be the same measurement, otherwise you will not have a squared quilt.

When the boards are in perfect alignment, tape them to the table with duct tape so that they will not move. Then mark cutting lines with a mechanical pencil or blue painters tape taped just inside the boards. Do not use the blue water-soluble marker because you will not be washing the quilt again and the marker could bleed into the rest of quilt.

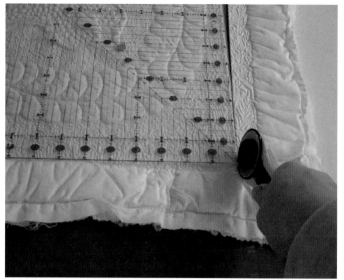

Remove the boards and slide a small rotary-cutting mat under the quilt. Using a square ruler and a 12" x 24" rotary ruler, cut along the drawn line or tape.

Binding

Cut 2⅛" bias strips from starched fabric and join with 45-degree angle seams. Press the seams open. Fold the binding in half lengthwise, wrong sides together, and press. Lay the binding around the quilt, roughly pinning it in place, to make sure none of the seams will be located at any of the corners. Remove the quilt from the blocking area. If it's a large quilt, set up tables or your ironing board around your sewing machine to hold the weight of the quilt while sewing on the binding.

The finished binding should be approximately the same width on the front and the back. Sew the binding on for 6", then stop and fold it to the back of the quilt. Measure the width of the binding on the front and back. The back binding should only be a 1/16" wider than the front so that it covers the line of stitching. If it is correct, tape a sticky pad to the sewing machine to indicate precisely where the edge of the quilt and binding should be as you sew. Keep the quilt snug to the sticky pad just to make sure you are sewing exactly the same size seam all around the quilt.

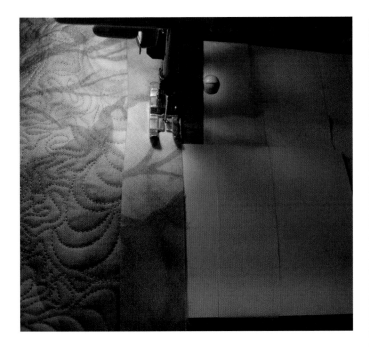

Sew to the corner and stop ¼" from the edge. Turn the quilt 90 degrees and backstitch off the edge.

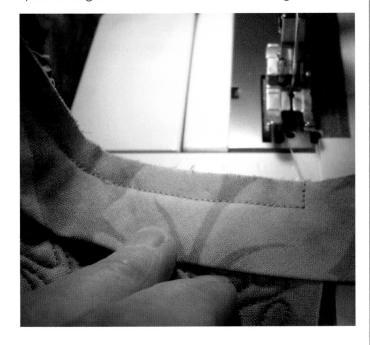

Fold the binding away from the quilt at a 45-degree angle, then fold back down along the next side of the quilt. Align the second fold with the edge of the quilt and the raw edges of the binding with the edge of the next side to be sewn. Continue around the quilt in the same manner.

Stop about 12" from where you started. Double-check the width of the binding on both sides. Resew any spots where the front and back widths aren't as they should be.

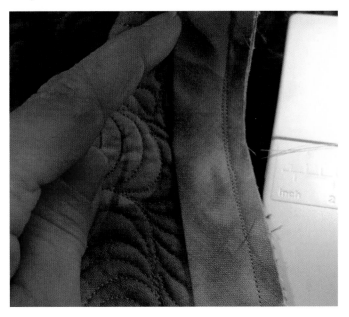

Fold back both ends of the binding so they just meet. Make a tiny cut about ¹/₁₆" at the folds to mark where the ends should connect.

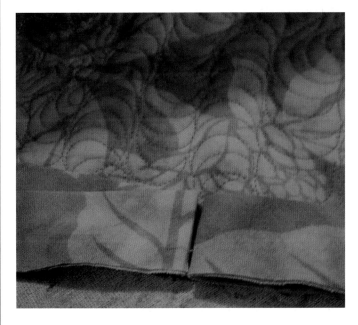

Finishing the Quilt

Open the binding, overlap the ends at right angles to each other, and pin along the sewing line, matching the tiny cuts.

Sew diagonally across the overlap, removing the pins as you go. Trim the seam and finger press it open. Refold, pin the binding along the edge, and sew in place.

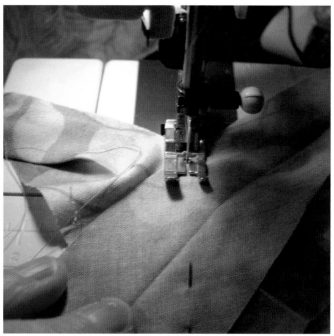

Fold the binding to the back of the quilt, forming a miter at the corners on the front and back. Pin the binding to the back of the quilt before you hand sew it, making sure you have a perfect miter on the back and on the front.

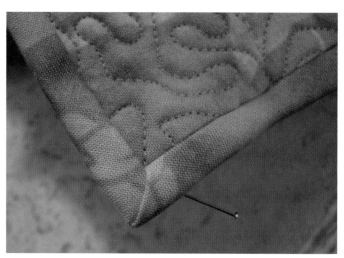

Hand stitch the binding in place.

During the finishing of the quilt I actually let the left side of my brain help me do a good job. The finishing touches of your quilt will reflect your professionalism.

Be proud of your work. You are an artist. You can do free-motion quilting with joy and skill. I will be in the back of your mind encouraging you. Happy Quilting!

esources

Quilters

Pam Clarke
Home Stitches
www.homestitches.com
Center stencils and pounce pads

Joan Davis
Gutzy Geisha Designs
Quilt Corral Too
23835 Highway 385
Hill City, SD 57745
www.quiltcorral.com

Diane Gaudynski
www.dianegaudynski.net
Quilt Savvy: Gaudynski's Machine Quilting Guidebook,
American Quilter's Society, 2006.

Renae Haddadin
www.renaequilts.com
Amazing Ways to Use Circles & Rays, American
Quilter's Society, 2010.

Karen McTavish
kmctavish@designerquilts.com
Mastering the Art of McTavishing, On-Word Bound
Books, 2005.
*The Secrets of Elemental Quilting: Innovative Quilting
Designs Plus Trapunto Tips & Tricks*, On-Word Bound
Books, 2006.
*Quilting for Show: A Practical Guide to Successful
Competition Quilting*, On-Word Bound Books, 2007.

Mary Sue Suit
www.msquilt.com
Crazy Eights: Fun with 8-Pointed Stars, Martingale and
Company, 2005.
A New Turn on Drunkard's Path, Martingale and
Company, 2002.
All the Blocks Are Geese: Flying Geese-the Fast Way,
That Patchwork Place, 1994.
A New Twist on Triangles, Martingale and Company,
1999.

Sharon Schamber
www.sharonschamber.com

Linda Taylor
www.thequiltingschool.com

Suppliers

Fil-Tec Bobbin Central
Embroidery and Quilting Solutions
www.bobbincentral.com

The Gadget Girls
www.thegadgetgirls.com
Shelly Zacharias

Golden Threads
www.goldenthreads.com
for Judy Allen's stencils

Judy Niemeyer
www.Quiltworx.com
Hawaiian Star pattern

King's Men Quilting Supply, Inc.
www.kmquiltingsupply.com
Towa Bobbin Case Tension Gauge

Red Rock Threads
www.redrockthreads.com

Pellon Batting
www.quiltlegacy.com

Quilter's Rule
www.quiltersrule.com

Superior Threads
www.superiorthreads.com

YLI Silk Thread
www.ylicorp.com

Books

Drawing on the Right Side of the Brain. Betty Edwards,
Tarcher, 1999.

Meet the Author

Judy is an internationally recognized, professional machine quilter whose quilts have won well over one hundred awards. With her piecing partners Mary Sue Suit and Joan Davis, she has won several first-place ribbons at such shows as the International Quilt Festival in Houston, shows sponsored by the American Quilter's Society, and the Machine Quilters Showcase.

She writes for many quilting magazines and has been featured on *The Quilt Show* with Alex Anderson and Ricky Tims. Hard work and a love of quilting have taken her from humble beginnings to an inspired quilter and teacher.

After growing up in Casper, Wyoming, she married her high school sweetheart and they raised five children. She was a busy stay-at-home mom until her baby, Melissa, entered pre-school. About that time her sister, Laura Bendrick, started making quilts. Judy was so motivated by her quilts that she started collecting fabric for her own quilts. She knew someday she would make quilts, but her life followed a different course.

She became a real estate broker and a five time top-listing agent. Her mother's death led Judy to make some life-changing decisions. She traded selling real estate for mortgage and agriculture lending, with less stress and more time with her children.

Her husband's job transfer found Judy in new employment as a chamber of commerce director of five small cities in Platte County, Wyoming. There she learned about helping other people start businesses. After another move, with the last child off to college, Judy finally found time to start quilting. She took her business start-up training from her chamber days and ordered a Gammill® quilting machine. "Every morning I get up, I can't wait to start quilting," she says.

Even though she has only been quilting for fifteen years, she has made up for lost time. Her ten-year friendship with best friend and motivator Mary Sue Suit pushed her to pursue teaching, lecturing, doing show quilts, and writing magazine articles while still quilting for customers. It took almost a lifetime, but she achieved her goals.

And behind everything she does is the loving support of her husband and children. "Life is good."

Visit Judy on her website:
www.judywoodworth.com

BUTTERFLY FANTASY
72½" x 72½". Made by the author.

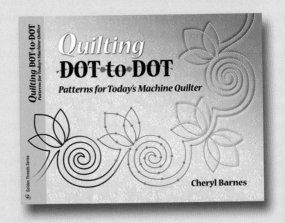
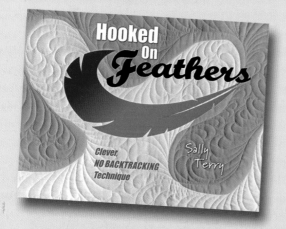
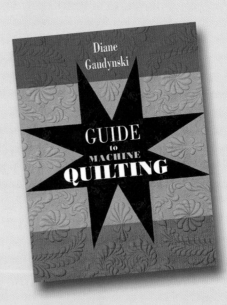
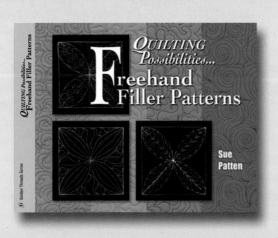